Dear Mama

100 LETTERS OF ENCOURAGEMENT FOR THE MILESTONES OF MOTHERHOOD

LAURA RADNIECKI

For Raleigh and River:
Being your mama and watching you grow
up is the greatest privilege of my life.
I love you both.

TABLE OF CONTENTS

LETTER #1

FOR YOU, WHEN YOU DECIDE TO START TRYING FOR A BABY

Dear Mama,

You've made the decision to start trying for a baby…

Chances are, even reading that sentence or saying the words out loud flood you with a whole range of emotions.

You feel excited, but also anxious at the same time. Nervous, but also happy.

It's… complicated.

Know this - whatever you are feeling, it's ok.

Every thought, every feeling, no matter what it is… it's ok, and you're allowed to feel it.

You can be excited to have a baby and scared at the same time.

You can be happy and hopeful, and anxious too.

You can be ready for the next chapter and grieving the end of an era too.

It's ok to be both, or none of it.

However you are feeling right now, and however you'll be feeling tomorrow or next week, give yourself grace.

It's going to be ok, and so are you.

In fact, it's going to be great.

LETTER #2

FOR YOU, WHEN YOU WONDER IF YOU ARE REALLY READY TO HAVE A BABY

Dear Mama,

It might have crossed your mind before you made the decision to try for a baby...

Or maybe it didn't cross your mind until you were actually pregnant.

But chances are, sooner or later a thought will cross your mind:

"Am I really ready to have a baby?"

"Am I really ready to be a mom?"

If you've been wondering whether or not you're ready to have a baby, or if you are ready for the monumental life changes that come with motherhood... give your anxious heart a hug.

Here's the truth...

Right now, you might not feel ready to have a baby.

You might not feel ready for motherhood.

You might not feel ready today, tomorrow, or maybe not even next week or next month.

But rest assured, you *will* be ready by the time your baby arrives.

You'll learn how to be a mother as soon as your child arrives to make you one.

Of this, you can be sure.

LETTER #3

FOR YOU, WHEN YOU GET THAT FIRST POSITIVE PREGNANCY TEST

Dear Mama,

You felt the curiosity... you silently wondered, *"Could I be???"*

Perhaps you noticed a little extra tenderness, some unusual fatigue, or a weird nausea wave that caught you by surprise.

Or maybe you've been counting, trying; waiting for months.

Praying, and hoping.

Whatever the circumstances, it's official - you got a positive pregnancy test... *You are pregnant!*

Take a deep breath.

Now, take another one.

It's true. *You are going to have a baby.*

This will probably be a pivotal moment you'll remember forever. Life might not ever feel quite the same after this.

This is the moment you know for sure there is another life growing inside of you.

This is the moment you know you are now a mother.

Soak it in. Revel in it.

Share your news. Or don't, if you'd rather not.

Either way, take a second to sit with the revelation and let it wash over you.

Be present in this milestone moment.

Memorize where you are right now when you found out you are pregnant.

And the biggest congratulations to you!

LETTER #4

FOR YOU, WHEN YOU WORRY ABOUT THE "WHAT IF'S" OF PREGNANCY

Dear Mama,

You are finding yourself lost in the *"what ifs"* of pregnancy lately.

A tightness grips your chest, and a heaviness sinks to your belly as you find yourself wondering...

"What if I'm not ready to be a mother?"

"What if I'm going to be a bad mother?"

"What if there is something wrong with the pregnancy?"

"What if I lose the baby?"

Whatever these *"what ifs"* are that plague your mind lately, they are trying to threaten your peace and steal your joy.

But they are also a normal part of the process too.

Something new is coming into your life, and things as you know it are about to change forever.

It's normal to feel anxious about it, and wonder what things are going to be like.

It's also normal to fear things you don't want to happen.

You are not alone in feeling this way.

Here lies the challenge... allowing the *"what ifs"* to pass through your mind without getting stuck there.

That's where your focus needs to be.

Acknowledge all of your thoughts, worries, and fears.

Pregnancy can be scary.

Major life changes can be scary.

But you don't have to dwell on all of the worries and fears; you don't have to get stuck with them.

Instead, give yourself a few moments to wonder *"what if?"*

Then send that thought on its way, and focus on the best possible outcome instead.

The future remains a mystery, and nothing is guaranteed.

But joy can be found in soaking up the present moment, and looking to the future with hope.

You can do this.

LETTER #5

FOR YOU, WHEN YOU REALIZE YOUR LIFE IS ABOUT TO CHANGE FOREVER

Dear Mama,

Your life as you know it is about to change forever... and you're not quite sure how you feel about it.

You are pregnant, and you're happy and excited about it.

You want to be a mother, and you know this is the next right step for you and your family.

But the life you've lived, at least in some ways, is about to come to an end.

Children change things.

Motherhood changes things.

It doesn't have to completely morph your life into something unrecognizable, but things are surely going to change.

It's ok to grieve the loss of what you've known up to now.

Life is going to change, and it may take awhile to get used to it.

In some ways, you will miss parts of your old life; the life you had before you became a mother.

But here's a secret... your new reality is going to be really great too.

The sacrifices in motherhood will be worth it.

You might not fully understand it yet, but every mother agrees.

One day, you'll look back and realize it became true for you too.

Sure, you might still miss some parts of your old life, like sleeping as late as you want and laying in bed watching TV all day.

You might miss the quiet and calm, and having complete control over your schedule and surroundings.

But you will also know motherhood is right where you are meant to be.

Your life IS going to change.

But it's going to be *so* worth it.

Letter #6

For you, when you face an infertility journey you never expected

Dear Mama,

When you decided to get pregnant, you probably thought it would happen easily.

Maybe you figured you'd have to try for a few months, but you never doubted it would happen eventually.

Here you are now... staring at another negative pregnancy test after another unsuccessful month trying for a baby.

And you're wondering why it's not happening for you.

Infertility is a sad, hard, and often lonely journey that no one expects to find themselves on.

I'm so sorry that you are on it too.

Know that you are *not* alone.

You may feel lonely and isolated, but millions of women have experienced the cruel sting of infertility before you and many will after you too.

You are not alone in this disappointment and sadness.

Also, this doesn't have to be where it stops.

This doesn't have to be the end of your journey to motherhood.

Resources are available, and options exist.

When you are ready, let those who have dedicated their careers to overcoming infertility help you get closer to your motherhood dream.

Let those who've also endured infertility offer you comfort and reassurance.

Let their eventual success give you hope.

Also, you are allowed to feel angry and sad that you have to know what infertility feels like.

You are allowed to grieve not having an easily-achieved pregnancy.

It's not fair.

But it doesn't have to be the end of your story.

Keep going.

You were made to be a mama and your future baby is waiting for you.

LETTER #7

Dear Mama,

You've been inducted into a club that you never wanted to join - the club of infertility.

It's a cruel club that carries feelings of hurt, fear, and loneliness.

It's a cruel club that leaves its members feeling broken, failing, and hopeless.

Anger overflows... especially when people get pregnant when they don't want to and surely aren't trying to.

That is the biggest gut-punch.

Someone's nightmare is another's dream.

It really is unfair.

Your anger is allowed.

Your anger is justified.

It's ok to be furious that you are facing infertility while others get pregnant when they don't want to.

It's ok to be furious that becoming a mother isn't as simple for you as a month or two of trying, followed by a positive pregnancy test.

But be careful with the anger; be careful of letting it damage your spirit.

Don't let your anger drown you.

Don't let it control what happens next in your story.

Acknowledge your anger, but don't let it overtake you.

Infertility doesn't have to be the end of your journey to motherhood.

Look into the resources; let the experts help you.

Your baby is waiting.

LETTER #8

Dear Mama,

It happened again.

You were scrolling through social media and you saw another pregnancy announcement.

Another post with cute props, smiling faces, and good news shared with the world.

Your heart sinks and your stomach tightens... Again.

It's so hard to see others getting what you so desperately want but haven't yet received.

It's hard to read, hard to hear, hard to celebrate; even when it's someone you love dearly and are truly happy for.

When you want something so bad and it's not happening yet, it is just plain hard to see others sharing their news..

15

It's ok to not look at social media for a while.

It's ok to disconnect to protect your tender heart.

It's ok to be happy for others but terribly sad for yourself, all at the same time.

It's ok, however you are feeling.

When you are praying for your own happy news, be kind to yourself.

When you hear someone else's happy news and fresh grief flows, show your weary spirit grace.

LETTER #9

FOR YOU, WHEN THERE IS NO HEARTBEAT

Dear Mama,

Maybe you were blindsided by the news.

Or maybe you had a feeling it was coming.

Whether you expected it or not, hearing those words *"I'm sorry. There is no heartbeat."* is a blow to the heart that hits in a way nothing else does.

Breathe in.

Breathe out.

Whatever you are feeling at this moment, just breathe.

Here are the undeniable facts.

First, *you are a mother.*

Heartbeat or no heartbeat, you were carrying a life and that makes you a mother - now and forevermore.

Second, you are not alone.

No one wants to join the group of mothers who have sat where you sit right now, but far too many have.

Millions of women have been in your shoes, and many will sadly be in the future.

You are not alone in your grief nor in your pain.

And third, there is no "right" way to feel or act after something like this happens.

(And if someone tells you otherwise, they are wrong.)

You get to decide how to grieve.

You get to decide how to mourn.

You get to decide how to remember.

And when you are ready, you get to decide how to move forward.

For now, be kind to yourself.

Be kind to your heart.

You are a mother.

Letter #10

For you, when you hear the unexpected - Twins!

Dear Mama,

You'll never forget that moment, will you?

The moment when a routine ultrasound reveals the shocking news that you are pregnant with not only ONE baby, but TWO!

Two babies.

Twins!

"Are you sure???"

"Yes, there are definitely two babies in there. Congratulations!"

Shock. Excitement. Disbelief. Happiness. Anxiousness.

Take a deep breath.

You feel overwhelmed by what this means for your pregnancy, delivery, and newborn phase.

You are struggling to wrap your brain around caring for two babies at once.

"Isn't one baby hard enough?!"

Here are the truths:

First, twin pregnancies are tricky and tough - carrying two babies challenges your body in unique ways.

But you are not the first twin mama-to-be, nor will you be the last.

Many have traveled this path before, and you will do great.

Second, twin deliveries are often different from single baby deliveries.

You are in good hands with your medical team. They will take good care of you.

Third, caring for two newborns at the same time is hard.

But you're not the first nor the last to do it successfully, and that should be encouraging.

You will find your way and you will be able to offer advice to new twin mamas one day.

So yes, having twins is a whole different ball game - much different than having one baby.

But, you can do this.

You WILL do this.

And one day, you'll be able to extend kindness, encouragement, and love to a shocked new mama who just found out she's having twins, because you have done it too.

LETTER #11

FOR YOU, WHEN YOU WORRY ABOUT YOUR PET BEING FORGOTTEN WHEN THE NEW BABY COMES

Dear Mama,

They were yours first.

Whether you rescued them or raised them, your pet was your first baby.

You've loved them, spoiled them, photographed them, and cared for them like a child. In every extent of the word, they are your *(fur)* child.

Your first baby.

Now that you are pregnant, you are experiencing conflicted emotions about your beloved pet.

Will they feel forgotten?

Will they BE forgotten?

Will they be able to adjust to the new family dynamics?

It's ok to wonder.

It's ok to worry.

After all, they were your first baby.

But rest assured, your love can cover both of them.

Things will change.

But they *(and you)* will be ok.

Your family will grow, and your heart will grow along with it.

LETTER #12

FOR YOU, WHEN YOU ARE PACKING YOUR HOSPITAL BAG

Dear Mama,

It's time to pack your hospital bag.

Maybe you're a last minute packer, and you're frantically throwing things into a duffel while you breathe through contractions.

Or perhaps you're getting an early start; trying to be prepared ahead of time in case you're surprised before your due date.

Either way, it's time to pack your hospital bag... and that makes it all feel so much more *real.*

Soon, you'll be heading to the hospital to have your baby.

Soon, you'll be welcoming your new baby into the world.

Soon, you'll be looking at the baby you've been wondering about for months; meeting them face to face... finally.

It's almost time.

For now, take a deep breath.

Calm the butterflies dancing in your stomach.

Quiet your racing mind and your rapid heartbeat.

Release the tension from your shoulders.

Whether you find yourself filled with excitement or anxiety *(or a strange mix of both),* know that it is all going to be ok.

Pack that hospital bag with eagerness and care.

Let it make you excited.

Good things are coming.

LETTER #13

FOR YOU, WHEN YOU FEEL LIKE YOU CAN'T POSSIBLY PUSH ONE MORE TIME

Dear Mama,

You are tired.

You are weary.

You are just plain worn out.

You've worked so hard for so long, and you're not sure you have anything left.

You feel like giving up.

Breathe in.

Breathe out.

You can do this.

You can finish what you started.

You can bring your baby into this world, and you *are* going to do it.

You can push another time.

You *will* push another time.

Dig deep.

Find the strength that's hidden deep inside of you, and use it.

Use that reservoir of strength to finish this.

One more push.

You are almost done.

You can do this.

LETTER #14

FOR YOU, WHEN YOU NEED TO HAVE A C-SECTION

Dear Mama,

Sometimes, the process doesn't go as planned.

Sometimes, despite your hardest, most valiant efforts, a change of plans is required for the safety of you and for the safety of your baby.

Sometimes, a c-section is needed.

Maybe it's a welcome relief after hours of stalled progress or scary, urgent complications.

Or maybe it's a heartbreaking detour to a thoughtfully crafted birth plan.

However the news of the c-section comes, know this:

You did not fail.

In fact, you sacrificed yourself for the safety of your baby.

And now, you have to care for your newborn as you're healing from major surgery yourself.

That is not inferior to giving birth vaginally.

That is *not* failure.

It's a sacrifice.

It's bravery.

It's love.

If you needed to have a c-section for the health and safety of yourself or your baby, you did not fail.

You'll forever have a scar to remind yourself of the sacrifice you made to bring your baby into the world.

You are a warrior.

LETTER #15

FOR YOU, WHEN YOU HEAR YOUR BABY CRY FOR THE FIRST TIME.

Dear Mama,

There's nothing quite like it - the sound of your newborn baby crying for the very first time.

Perhaps you were holding your breath and you didn't even realize it.

But as soon as you heard that precious, brand new cry, the exhale came and maybe the tears too.

Your baby is here.

Your baby is safe.

Listen to that throaty, loud sound that is music from the heavens, and let it fill your heart with joy.

You did it.

You brought your baby into the world.

Your baby is here.

Congratulations!

LETTER #16

FOR YOU, WHEN YOU HOLD YOUR BABY FOR THE FIRST TIME

Dear Mama,

Have you pictured what it will be like?

Have you envisioned what it will feel like when your new baby is placed into your arms?

All the day-dreaming in the world can't quite prepare you for that sacred moment when you hold your brand new baby for the very first time.

Maybe your baby is laid on your chest, moments after delivery.

Perhaps they are wrapped in a blanket, and brought to your cheek for that first sweet hello during a c-section.

Or, for mamas with babies in the NICU, it could be hours or days later, with a delicate dance navigating cords and tubes.

However it happens and whatever the circumstances, the moment when you get to hold your new baby for the very first time is a core memory you will remember forever.

Take a deep breath.

Pause and pay attention.

"Hello sweet baby."

"I am your mama."

"It's so good to meet you."

"We are so happy you're here."

LETTER #17

Dear Mama,

Maybe you went to a breastfeeding class, or talked with a lactation consultant.

Maybe you have friends who shared their experiences with you, or you researched it yourself.

Despite how ready you are, nothing quite prepares you for this raw experience of motherhood.

Tears may come to your eyes as you witness a dream fulfilled.

Or maybe your brain is still foggy from delivery and you're letting the nurse make it happen this time.

Your baby might latch right away, or it may take a few tries and different positions to make it work.

It might feel weird and even hurt the first time.

Don't panic.

Don't overcomplicate it.

Enjoy it, if it's a happy moment for you.

If it's not a great moment this time, trust that it'll get better.

Breastfeeding your baby is a journey; a process.

For now, relax and rest.

You've done the extraordinary hard work of bringing your baby here.

LETTER #18

FOR YOU, WHEN YOU EAT YOUR FIRST MEAL AFTER DELIVERY

Dear Mama,

Labor often comes with lots of rules about what you can eat and when.

The rules are based on science and precaution, but sometimes it's just plain rough.

Once labor is over and delivery is done, the rules lift.

Your appetite returns.

And then, it's time to eat.

Maybe you've been sick your entire pregnancy.

Maybe your favorite foods haven't sounded or tasted good in months.

Maybe you have been dreaming of your post-delivery meal in such vivid detail, you can smell it and taste it.

It's time.

You've earned it.

Whatever you crave, now is the time to eat it.

Big, juicy burger? Sure.

A giant pizza? Great.

Some random mix of weird things that somehow sound like the most delicious meal on the planet? Wonderful!

Whatever your heart and your appetite desires, let yourself savor a well-deserved meal.

You brought life into this world.

Dig in!

LETTER #19

FOR YOU, WHEN YOU GET UP TO WALK FOR THE FIRST TIME AFTER A C-SECTION

Dear Mama,

C-section mothers are rockstars.

A c-section is major surgery that happens while you're awake.

And afterwards, you're expected to get out of bed mere hours later, and learn to care for a newborn baby whose life literally depends on you.

Anyone who thinks c-sections are the easy route have clearly never had one.

If you've had a c-section birth, the time will come when the nurse walks into your room to help you get out of bed for the first time after your surgery.

You might not be able to fathom moving, much less getting out of bed.

But you can do this.

The sooner you get up out of bed and begin to move around *(no matter how slowly)*, the sooner your recovery can begin.

Getting up out of bed will help you get clean.

Getting up out of bed will help your healing.

Getting up out of bed will make you feel a bit more normal.

Your nurse will help you.

It will hurt, and you'll be sore, but you will be ok.

You can do this.

Slowly, steadily, one step at a time.

You've got this.

LETTER #20

FOR YOU, WHEN YOU TAKE YOUR FIRST SHOWER AFTER DELIVERY

Dear Mama,

Showers are a magnificent thing.

You are about to experience the most profound shower of your life.

After an intense, exhausting delivery bringing your newborn baby into this world, the simple joy of a shower is unmatched.

After a c-section and bravely standing up for the first time after major surgery, the simple joy of a shower is unlike anything you've experienced before.

This time, a shower isn't just a shower.

It's victory.

It's a triumph.

It's earned, deserved, and needed.

Let the water wash away anything leftover from your battle to bring your baby to earth.

Let the water lift your heart, and remind you of the feat you just accomplished.

Let the water renew your spirit, if you're feeling tired or weary.

Your baby is here.

You did it.

You are a mother.

LETTER #21

Dear Mama,

Maybe you grew up with younger siblings.

Maybe you did a lot of babysitting, and changed many diapers in your youth.

Or perhaps neither is true, and you've never changed a baby's diaper in your entire life.

Regardless of your history with changing diapers, your baby is here and you are about to change their diaper for the very first time.

It might feel weird or even scary at first.

They are so little.

So wiggly.

The diapers are so small.

But you can do this.

It doesn't have to be elegant.

It doesn't matter how you do it, as long as you get the old one off, your baby gets clean, and you get the new one on.

Laugh a little; find the humor in it.

This is the first of many, many diaper changes in your future.

It will become less awkward.

You'll be a diaper-changing whiz in no time.

LETTER #22

FOR YOU, WHEN YOU GET FAMILIAR WITH YOUR BABY'S NAME

Dear Mama,

Who knew naming your baby would be so hard??

So many options, so many possibilities.

Or maybe for you, it wasn't hard at all.

Maybe you knew exactly what your baby would be named, and never second-guessed it.

Either way, a name is somewhat abstract until it's paired with a face.

With a body.

With a being.

Calling your new baby by their name for the first time is a magical experience.

It might even be a little bit odd too - it's like meeting someone for the first time and getting used to their name.

Every time you say the name you selected especially for them, it will become a little more familiar; a little more *"theirs."*

One day soon, you'll look at them and know they were never meant to be called anything else.

Their name will just fit.

Letter #23

For you, when you leave the
hospital for the first time

Dear Mama,

It's almost time.

Your bags are packed, the discharge paperwork has been signed, and you're ready to go.

It's time to put your baby in the car seat for the very first time, and leave the hospital.

You'll check the car seat buckles several times.

Maybe you'll opt to ride in the back and sit next to your baby.

As you pull away from the hospital, you'll probably be flooded with a mix of emotions.

Joy and excitement to go home to your own space.

Perhaps there's a layer of anxiety and fear there too - maybe even a little incredulity.

"This baby is now solely in our care!"

"We have no idea what we are doing!?"

"Help!"

Take a deep breath.

This is uncharted territory.

It's scary and weird and nerve-wracking.

But it's also gloriously wonderful.

You are taking your new baby *home*.

You will do great.

Your baby will do great.

You will do great together.

LETTER #24
FOR YOU, WHEN YOUR MILK COMES IN

Dear Mama,

You know what to expect when your milk comes in, but it's one of those things that has to be experienced to truly understand it.

You'll know when it starts.

You'll be surprised and maybe even weirded out by the sudden changes in your breasts; you thought you knew well.

It's remarkable how hard they can get.

It's strange.

It's weird.

It's amazing.

And it will settle and stabilize soon.

Engorgement won't last forever.

The intense hardness won't last forever.

The pain won't last forever.

Your body is ready to feed that little baby of yours and help them grow.

The miracle of life continues.

You are doing a great job.

LETTER #25

FOR YOU, WHEN YOUR NIPPLES FEEL LIKE THEY ARE ON FIRE

Dear Mama,

Breastfeeding is hard.

Some people say it's natural, magical, and the most intense bonding experience ever.

And sometimes, it is.

But other times, it's not.

Other times, it's just plain hard.

Until you've tried to breastfeed a baby, you likely didn't pay much attention to your nipples.

And you probably don't have too much experience with cracked, bleeding, sore nipples.

But breastfeeding...

Breastfeeding can turn normal nipples into sore, cracked, bloody messes that can bring tears to your eyes.

Seek out help; lactation consultants are there for you.

Try different positions. Try different creams or balms.

And if you need to, try formula to give your body a break.

Giving your baby formula doesn't mean breastfeeding is over; you can use formula and breastfeed too.

Remember that fed is best; a full belly is the best gift you can give to your baby.

That, and a healthy, sane mama.

Be kind to yourself.

Take things one day at a time.

LETTER #26

FOR YOU, WHEN YOUR BABY IS CLUSTER FEEDING

Dear Mama,

Cluster feeding.

You've likely heard of it, and probably even know what it is.

But it might not dawn on you, when you're holding a rooting baby for the 3rd time in an hour, wondering how on earth they want to eat again.

"They just nursed 10 minutes ago!?"

If this sounds like you, your baby might be cluster feeding.

They might be teaching your body how much milk to produce.

Resist the urge to assume your baby isn't getting enough milk.

"If they were getting enough, how could they possibly be hungry already?!"

Resist the urge to read too much into what's happening.

Resist the urge to panic.

Try to read your baby.

Try to go with their flow.

Try to feed when they signal for it, at least for a little while.

Cluster feeding won't last forever.

LETTER #27

FOR YOU, WHEN YOU ARE SO TIRED, YOU FEEL LIKE YOU MIGHT DIE

Dear Mama,

Your eyes are heavy and your brain is foggy.

Your bones are achy and your soul is weary.

Your arms are tired and your emotions are wild.

You are exhausted.

You are sleep deprived.

When asked what the hardest part of new motherhood is, many women say the lack of sleep, and for good reason.

Sleep is essential.

Sleep is like oxygen.

But in the early days with a new baby, sleep is also elusive.

Sleep becomes a distant memory… at least temporarily.

There will be times when you are so tired, you just want to bawl.

There will be times when you are so tired, you feel like you could actually die.

But you won't.

It's amazing how resilient your body actually is.

It's amazing how much your body can endure.

Here's a promise to you:

One day, you WILL sleep again.

The disrupted sleep of the newborn phase won't last forever.

The chaotic sleep pattern your baby has right now won't always be this way.

The extreme exhaustion, the kind you feel deep in your bones, won't last forever.

It's going to get better.

Keep going.

LETTER #28

Dear Mama,

It's the middle of the night, and you're awake - again.

Maybe it's midnight or maybe it's 4 am, but the darkness is the same, and the exhaustion is too.

The rest of your house is asleep, but not you.

And not your baby.

You two are up - *again* - and you're feeding - *again*.

The middle of the night can feel like one of the loneliest times of your life.

In the middle of the night, your house can feel like the darkest, most isolated place on the planet, and you feel certain no one else on Earth is awake at this hour.

You are not alone.

Right now, another mama is sitting alone in the dark, feeding her baby and begging for just a few more minutes of sleep.

Right now, another mama is crying tears of exhaustion, wondering how she can possibly stay awake another second longer.

Right now, mamas all over the world are awake, in the middle of the night, feeding their babies, just like you.

You are not alone.

You are tired, you are weary, and you are lonely.

But you are not alone.

You are *never* alone.

Letter #29

For you, when you give your baby their first bottle of formula

Dear Mama,

Sometimes life doesn't go as planned.

Despite breastfeeding prep classes, all the right products and tools, and even the best help available…

Sometimes, breastfeeding doesn't come easily.

For some, breastfeeding doesn't work at all.

The day may come when your baby needs formula.

This can feel like a monumental failure.

A travesty.

After all, *"breast is best,"* right?

Well, yes, breast milk is wonderful.

But, a *fed* baby beats everything else.

If the day comes when your baby needs formula for any reason, give that baby the formula.

And let any guilt go.

A fed baby is what matters.

A healthy, happy mama is what matters.

If breastfeeding is causing stress and worry, the benefits may not be worth it.

If breastfeeding is interfering with you caring for your baby in the way you want to, it might not be worth it.

It's ok to give that bottle of formula.

It doesn't mean you failed at anything.

It means you are going to fill your baby's belly.

It means you are going to have a content, fed baby.

It simply means you are a good mother.

LETTER #30

FOR YOU, WHEN TEARS COME TO YOUR EYES FOR THE TENTH TIME THIS HOUR

Dear Mama,

Here they come again...

The tears.

Suddenly, your throat gets tight and your eyes fill up.

What triggered it this time?

Maybe there wasn't even a trigger. Maybe the tears just came.

When you feel like you've cried 10 times in the last hour, give yourself permission to cry again.

The tears may come; let them fall.

The early days after having a baby will put you on a rollercoaster of emotions unlike anything you've experienced before.

The hormones you hear about are a real thing.

You might cry from love, happiness, joy, exhaustion, pain, anxiety, or any other emotion you can think of.

Or maybe, you'll just cry for no identifiable reason at all.

And that's ok too.

When the tears come, let them fall.

It won't be like this forever.

But for now?

Let them fall.

You will be ok.

LETTER #31

Dear Mama,

You learned about it in birth class.

But that was in theory; now it's happening to you.

Baby blues.

Postpartum depression.

How do you tell the difference?

How do you know when baby blues cross the line into postpartum depression?

How do you know when you need help?

If you find yourself asking this question, it's worth asking a trusted expert about it.

If your symptoms make you question whether they are baby blues or something worse, it's time to visit with your doctor.

If you have a hunch you're experiencing more than baby blues, you might be right.

Have a talk with your doctor.

Maybe it is the baby blues; at least you'll know.

And if it's crossing over into postpartum depression?

You can address that too.

No one should have to worry and wonder on their own.

Not when there are allies waiting and willing to help navigate this postpartum season.

Let them help you too.

LETTER #32
FOR YOU, WHEN YOU GRIEVE YOUR OLD LIFE

Dear Mama,

You miss your old life.

The no-kids, sleep-in, do-whatever-you-want life.

The predictable, tidy, quiet life.

Maybe you miss it a lot, or maybe just a little.

Don't feel guilty for it.

It doesn't mean you wish you'd never had a baby.

It doesn't mean you don't love your child.

It doesn't mean you're a bad mom.

Every parent misses their old life at one time or another.

(And if they say they don't, they're lying.)

Every mother misses the quiet, calm, tidy pre-kid life sometimes.

Especially when their child is crying, making a mess, or acting like a tornado.

You are a good mom.

And, you are doing a great job.

LETTER #33

FOR YOU, WHEN YOU DON'T FEEL LIKE YOU AT ALL

Dear Mama,

The postpartum phase can be really, really hard.

Just recently, your body literally pushed a whole human out of it.

Or if you had a c-section, your body was cut open through several different layers so your baby could be born, and then you were stitched back up, only to get out of bed and walk around just hours later.

You lost a large amount of weight in a matter of minutes, and your once-hard belly is now a squishy, malleable blob.

You are bleeding from places that haven't bled in months, and if you had any further complications, you have even more challenges to deal with.

Plus, you may be learning how to breastfeed your baby which brings with it a whole slew of new experiences, not all of which are pleasant.

Add in the sleep deprivation and exhaustion that comes with a newborn, and *good grief...*

Is it any wonder that the postpartum phase feels like walking around in a foreign body, on a foreign planet, trying to take care of an alien, when you haven't slept in a week?

When you don't feel like yourself in any way, shape or form, here's what you need to know...

This is temporary.

It feels like you'll never be *you* again, but that's not true.

You won't feel this off balance forever.

You won't feel this clueless forever.

You won't feel this exhausted forever.

You won't feel this sore, this weird, or this gross forever.

The postpartum phase will pass.

Your body will stop bleeding and hurting.

You will find your footing.

Your baby will sleep again.

YOU will sleep again.

And one day soon, you'll wake up and realize, *"Hey, I feel a little bit like me again."*

What a beautiful day that will be.

LETTER #34

FOR YOU, WHEN YOUR HOUSE/HAIR/CLOTHES/DISHES ARE DIRTY, AND YOU FEEL LIKE A FAILURE

Dear Mama,

A new baby throws everyone and everything for a loop; old rhythms of life go out the window.

It can be an extra cruel type of chaos for routine-loving, type-A mamas.

A new baby means change.

A new baby means pressing pause on a tidy house, clean laundry, or completed to-do list.

A new baby means everything else becomes the last priority, for now.

When your house is dirty, your sink is full, and you haven't showered in who knows how long, cut yourself some slack.

When you feel like a total failure, give yourself grace.

Is your baby eating, sleeping, and using up diapers?

Are you eating and sleeping as much as you can?

If those two answers are yes, you are doing a great job.

For routine-loving, type-A mamas, letting the laundry pile up or the dishes fill the sink can feel like an impossible task.

Try your hardest to put blinders on and let them be... *for now*.

You will be able to clean again soon.

You will be able to keep up with the laundry again soon.

You will be able to do more than just feed, sleep, change diapers, and repeat... soon.

For now, turn your attention to your baby.

Soon, you'll have capacity for more.

Letter #35
For you, when you feel like routine will never return

Dear Mama,

A new baby flips your world upside down.

You fall head over heels in love with a new person you just met, and your routine and schedule change completely.

Babies don't know what time it is.

Babies don't know what day it is.

Babies don't care about anyone's schedule; they just want their needs met.

This is hard for routine-focused people.

This is hard for people who like predictability, productivity, and control.

In the early postpartum days, there is no schedule.

There is no predictability.

There is no planning.

It's just you, your baby, and doing the very best you can.

Hour by hour, and sometimes minute by minute.

It won't always be this way; things won't always be so chaotic.

One day soon, you'll realize your baby is forming a nap pattern.

You'll notice a pattern forming with feeding times too.

You'll realize you know what the next few hours look like, and you can predict when you'll be awake at night.

One day soon, you'll look around and say, *"Hey, we have a routine now."*

Until then, hang on.

The newborn chaos is temporary.

LETTER #36

FOR YOU, WHEN YOU FEEL LIKE YOU ARE BARELY KEEPING YOUR HEAD ABOVE WATER

Dear Mama,

Motherhood is hard.

Recovering from birth is hard.

Caring for a baby is hard.

Change is hard.

Life feels upside down right now, and you barely feel like you can keep your head above water.

You're furiously treading water and you're not sure how long you can keep it up.

Keep going... just for a little bit longer.

The postpartum phase is hard, but it gets better.

Change is hard.

But eventually, things become familiar again.

Keep going.

Things are going to get better.

LETTER #37

FOR YOU, WHEN YOU FEEL LIKE YOU'LL NEVER SLEEP AGAIN

Dear Mama,

There is *"tired"* and then there is *"bone-deep exhaustion."*

The haven't-slept-for-months-and-no-end-in-sight level of tiredness that dulls the senses, heightens the emotions, and makes you wonder how you can possibly endure.

This is the type of tiredness that accompanies a new baby.

When you swear you'll *never, ever, ever* sleep again...

You will.

One day, your baby will sleep through the night.

One day, your first thought when you wake up will no longer be, *"I'm so exhausted. When do I get to sleep again?"*

One day, you will sleep through the night again, too.

For now, hang on.

Sleep when you can.

Rest your eyes when you can't sleep.

Even when you feel like you are so tired you might die, you won't.

And one day soon, you WILL sleep again.

LETTER #38

FOR YOU, WHEN YOU ARE COVERED IN SPIT-UP... AGAIN

Dear Mama,

How many outfits have you gone through today?

How many times have you been covered in spit up *(or pee, or poop, or heck... all of them at the same time?)*

Maybe you've lost count, or you've given up keeping track.

When you find yourself covered in spit up *again*, know that it won't always be this way.

Most babies spit up a little bit.

Some babies spit up a lot.

But all babies eventually stop.

You might have 4 burp rags tucked into the pockets of your diaper bag right now, and another one hanging over your shoulder.

But one day, not too far from now, you'll suddenly realize that you've had the same burp rag in your diaper bag for weeks, and you haven't even needed to use it.

You'll wear the same shirt for an entire day, and not get a single stain on it.

One day soon, spit up will be a thing of the past, and you'll be thinking about potty training and loose baby teeth.

But right now, keep those burp rags nearby.

Use them.

Wash them.

And use them again.

Thank your lucky stars for your washing machine, and put another load in.

Most of all, rest assured that this too won't last forever.

LETTER #39

FOR YOU, WHEN YOU ARE TEMPTED TO CONSULT DR. GOOGLE AGAIN

Dear Mama,

There is one doctor you should stay away from.

Dr. Google.

You'll want to look up this symptom or that rash.

You'll want to ask how long something will last.

You'll want to search whether something is normal or not.

You'll be tempted so many times, sometimes multiple times in the same day.

Don't give in.

Ask your questions to a trusted doctor who knows your child.

Dr. Google might have information for you, but it also opens the gates of worry, false diagnoses, drama, and anxiety... things you don't need on your already-full plate.

When Dr. Google beckons, put your phone in a drawer.

Save the questions for your pediatrician.

LETTER #40

FOR YOU, WHEN YOU BABYWEAR FOR THE FIRST TIME

Dear Mama,

Babywearing is something women have done for millennia, and now it's your turn.

Wraps, slings, structured carriers... There are dozens of different babywearing options.

You get to decide what type you try.

The feeling of wearing your baby snug to your chest, close to your heart, is unmatched.

It connects you to your baby in a primal way.

They are nestled safely against you.

They are close enough to kiss.

They are calm.

And the best part?

Your hands are free.

Enjoy wearing your baby.

Enjoy wrapping them up and tying them snuggly to your chest.

Enjoy tightening the sling and feeling them settle into just the right spot.

Clip the carrier and tighten the straps.

Decide how you want to carry them - front, hip, back or any of the other variations.

Enjoy the process, and cherish the closeness.

Babywearing is precious and it is fleeting.

Soak it up.

LETTER #41

FOR YOU, WHEN YOU TAKE YOUR BABY ON AN ERRAND FOR THE FIRST TIME

Dear Mama,

Remember the days when you simply grabbed your purse and keys, and headed to Target?

No planning, no packing.

Who knew going to Target with a baby could be such a big production?!

One day, a spontaneous Target trip will be possible again, but not today.

Today, you are packing your diaper bag, trying to think of everything you might possibly need for this first outing to run errands.

Right now, you are stashing diapers, wipes, burp rags, toys, and anything else you can think of in all of the pockets and compartments, hoping you remembered everything.

Right now, the process of leaving the house and getting to Target will take much longer than the actual shopping trip inside Target will.

Or maybe it's just a car ride because you're doing Target pickup!

In that case, you're a genius, and hopefully it'll be quick and easy.

As you prepare to head out on your first errands run with your new baby, take heart...

It won't always be this cumbersome, awkward, and time-consuming to run errands.

It won't always make you feel exhausted before you reach a single store.

It will get easier and it will get faster.

But for today, take a deep breath.

Don't forget to pack a few snacks for yourself...

And, go run those errands.

LETTER #42

FOR YOU, WHEN YOUR BABY SMILES AT YOU FOR THE FIRST TIME

Dear Mama,

The first few weeks of caring for a newborn are unlike anything else on this Earth.

You heal from delivery while experiencing massive changes both inside and outside your body.

All the while, you are learning to feed and care for a brand new baby, and you're barely sleeping.

It seems like all your baby does is eat, sleep, poop, pee, burp, and cry. And probably spit up too.

Motherhood is very one-sided at first.

You will give, and give, and give some more.

Your baby will snuggle as they sleep on your chest or in your arms, but early motherhood often feels very demanding and lopsided.

Until one day.

One day, your baby will look at you, and smile for the very first time.

One day, your baby will smile at you and that precious moment will be seared into your memory forever.

Soon, they'll follow the smile with a giggle.

From then on, things won't feel so lopsided anymore.

It won't feel like a one-sided relationship anymore.

You'll still be the one feeding, diapering, and caring for them... but they are giving you those precious smiles and giggles in return.

And it's remarkable how far they can go.

LETTER #43

FOR YOU, WHEN YOU HEAR YOUR BABY'S LAUGH FOR THE FIRST TIME

Dear Mama,

There are many beautiful sounds on this planet.

Waves rolling onto a sandy shore, rain tapping on a roof, birds chirping in the early morning light.

Lots of sounds make you stop and take notice; some even take your breath away.

But nothing compares to the sound of your baby laughing for the very first time.

That sound, *that sweet, precious sound,* cuts straight through you and touches your heart in a way nothing before it has.

The way your baby giggles will be seared into the deepest parts of your memory, forever.

Their laugh will brighten your day, lift your mood, and make your own face transform into a smile and laugh, even if it's 3 am and you haven't slept in hours.

Hearing your baby laugh is a sound so pure, so
precious, you will never, ever forget it.

Make sure to take a video of it too, just to be safe.

LETTER #44

FOR YOU, WHEN YOU CAN'T WAIT FOR YOUR BABY'S BEDTIME, BUT SCROLL THROUGH PHOTOS OF THEM SHORTLY AFTERWARDS

Dear Mama,

At the end of a long day, bedtime is the light at the end of the tunnel.

After hours of feeding, cleaning, wiping, clothing, washing, caring, soothing, and more, you are all done.

Your fuse is short.

Your energy bucket is empty.

You are so exhausted, you could bawl.

Is it bedtime yet?

You can't wait for the blissful moment when your child is sound asleep and you can take a big, deep breath.

Ahhhhhh.

But something weird happens...

You start to miss them.

You couldn't wait for them to go to bed, but as soon as they're asleep, you're suddenly looking through your phone at photos of them.

They're only in the other room, but you really do miss them.

It's a weird feeling, isn't it?

Motherhood is strange.

You are completely normal.

It's because you love them so much.

Look at those photos, and watch them sleep on the baby monitor.

Go peek at them and give them one last kiss if you want to.

But then, rest.

Relax.

Recover.

Enjoy a minute to yourself.

Tomorrow, it starts over again.

LETTER #45

FOR YOU, WHEN YOU ARE IN THE AWKWARD STAGE BETWEEN MATERNITY AND YOUR NORMAL CLOTHES

Dear Mama,

You aren't pregnant anymore.

After 9 months of pregnancy, that's a weird feeling, isn't it?

One minute you were pregnant, and the next, you're not anymore!

The thing is, your body took 9 months to grow a baby, so it won't return to its pre-baby size in a day.

It simply can't.

In the days following delivery, your body will change.

Your rock-hard baby belly will deflate and turn soft.

Your breasts will grow and fill.

All of the extra blood and fluid that filled your body to keep your baby alive will be eliminated.

Slowly but surely, your body will start to change.

For a while, you will be in the strange middle phase where maternity clothes no longer fit, but your pre-pregnancy clothes don't fit either.

It's a strange place to be.

Add to it that you're probably still healing from delivery, and you likely have at least one spit-up stain on your shirt at all times.

New motherhood is anything but glamorous.

Every day, things change a bit more.

This awkward middle phase is temporary; it won't last forever.

In the meantime?

Go buy one or two outfits that fit great right now.

Whatever size you are today, buy something that fits well.

You probably won't be able to wear it very long.

Soon, it'll probably be too big.

But right now?

It will fit well, and you'll feel good in it.

This postpartum phase is awkward enough without adding uncomfortable, unflattering clothing to the mix.

Buy something that fits well and makes you happy.

Wear it often.

And when it no longer fits, pass it on to someone else.

It has served its purpose.

It helped you through the messy middle.

It helped you get to the other side of pregnancy and the postpartum phase.

LETTER #46

FOR YOU, WHEN YOU RETURN TO WORK

Dear Mama,

Your maternity leave is over.

It's time for you to go back to work.

The date has been in the back of your mind, and now it's here.

How do you feel about it?

Are you ready?

Are you craving a little bit of normalcy; a little bit of your "old" life?

It's ok if you are.

After the immense change you've gone through, a glimmer of routine can feel a little like returning home.

But your heart feels heavy at the thought of leaving your newborn baby too.

Your eyes are misty, and your throat feels tight.

You are wondering how you're going to manage dropping them off and driving away.

It's ok... that's normal too.

It's ok to feel thrilled and devastated to return to work, all at the same time.

Your baby is going to be alright.

You are going to be alright.

LETTER #47

FOR YOU, WHEN YOU DROP YOUR BABY OFF AT DAYCARE FOR THE FIRST TIME

Dear Mama,

You did it.

You walked to the front door of your baby's daycare.

You swallowed the lump in your throat, blinked away the tears in your eyes, and handed your baby over to the *(carefully vetted)* caregiver for the very first time.

You said one more *"I love you"* and gave one more kiss, and then you turned and walked out the door for the very first time.

Maybe it felt impossible, and you cried as you drove away…

But you did it.

Whether you are returning to work, going back to school, or giving yourself a solo day for errands and space to breathe, you successfully dropped your baby off at daycare for the first time.

Now, the day is yours; go use it.

And at the end of the day, your reunion will be sweet.

LETTER #48

FOR YOU, WHEN YOU JUST NEED A BREAK

Dear Mama,

You've probably heard the quote before, but until you're a parent you don't fully understand it.

Having a child literally means a part of your heart is walking around outside your body.

When they are happy, you find your heart soaring.

When they are hurting, you feel their pain too.

You want to hug them and kiss them over and over, because you love them so much.

But also... *parenting is exhausting.*

Parenting requires immense energy, patience, and intentional thought.

Sometimes, you need a break.

Sometimes, you need peace and quiet.

Sometimes, you need to put yourself first and give yourself a minute.

Whether you accomplish that by passing your baby to your partner, hiring a babysitter, or ducking into a quiet spot when your baby is safely occupied, take a break.

You deserve it.

You need it.

LETTER #49

Dear Mama,

No one tells you the only outfits you need for the beginning of your baby's life are sleepers and onesies.

Stores are full of cute, tiny baby clothes, and they are frequent gifts at baby showers.

Teeny tiny sweaters, jeans, socks, and even miniature shoes... How can you resist?!

But those first few weeks of newborn life are a blur... a sleep-deprived, survival-mode, pee-poop-spit-up-soaked blur of adjustment.

When your baby spits up after every feeding, you have to change 10 diapers a day, and you rarely leave the house, why bother with a sweater and jeans?

Sleepers and onesies are the outfits of choice in those early weeks.

No one tells you the significance of dressing your baby in real clothes for the very first time, either.

The first time you dress your baby in an actual outfit causes a visceral reaction inside your heart.

Suddenly, you can picture your teeny baby as a toddler.

Maybe even as a little kid.

All of a sudden, your tiny baby becomes a little kid in front of your eyes.

For a tender mama heart, it can serve as a rude awakening - an immensely cute awakening, but rude nonetheless.

Who knew sweaters and jeans had such power?

Take pictures of that first true outfit.

Look a little closer at how their sweet face looks, framed in that sweater.

Sear the image of them wearing itty bitty jeans into your memory.

You want to remember the moment when you first got a glimpse of your baby as a kid.

All thanks to a tiny sweater and a pair of jeans.

LETTER #50

FOR YOU, WHEN YOU FEEL LIKE YOU HAVE NO IDEA WHAT THE HECK YOU ARE DOING

Dear Mama,

Take a big inhale.

Now let it out, slowly.

Do it again.

In... out...

Parenting is hard.

Very hard, sometimes.

There are times when you feel like you're excelling at it; doing everything right and everything is going smoothly.

Then suddenly, things shift and you feel like you have absolutely no idea what the heck you're doing.

We've all been there.

You are not alone.

Here's a little secret - *none* of us know what we're doing.

Sometimes we have peaceful, calm days, and other times, we end the day sobbing into our pillow, wondering how we can possibly do it all over again, tomorrow.

No one has it all figured out.

Cherish the days that go smoothly; the days where things went great.

Use those memories as proof you're doing something right.

And those bad days when you have no clue what you're doing?

Breathe...

Keep going.

Every morning is a fresh start.

Take things one step at a time, one day at a time.

And remember... *no one* knows what they're doing

LETTER #51

FOR YOU, WHEN YOUR BABY ROLLS OVER FOR THE FIRST TIME

Dear Mama,

You've spent months watching your baby lay on their back or on their belly.

They have squirmed, wiggled, and practiced lifting their head during tummy time...

But they never rolled over.

Until today.

Today, your little baby rolled over for the very first time.

Did you see it happen?

Or did you look over and see they were facing a different direction than they were before?

It happens so fast!

This is the beginning of your baby using rolling to get around.

This is the start of motion.

LETTER #52

FOR YOU, WHEN YOUR BABY CRAWLS FOR THE FIRST TIME

Dear Mama,

You've been cheering your baby on for months.

First, they rolled one way, and then the other.

Pretty soon, they could roll all over the floor.

Next, they worked their way up to their hands and knees, and then rocked back and forth.

You've watched, you've cheered, and you've probably coaxed too.

They weren't quite ready yet.

Today, they were ready.

Today, your baby crawled for the very first time.

You officially have a crawler!

A new phase begins.

LETTER #53

FOR YOU, WHEN YOUR BABY TAKES THEIR FIRST STEP

Dear Mama,

You've experienced lots of firsts with your baby so far.

First breastfeeding session, first diaper change, first smile, first giggle, first time rolling over, first time crawling.

All of these firsts took your breath away in their own unique way, and made you stop and commit them to memory.

But there's always been one major milestone up ahead, in the future.

You knew it was coming.

You know the general time frame when it usually happens.

Yet, despite how prepared you think you are, that milestone has the power to take your breath away and almost bring you to your knees.

That moment is your baby's first steps.

Your baby has been walking while holding onto furniture for awhile.

They've been toddling around while holding onto your hands.

But this is different.

This is unassisted, intentional, on-two-legs, brave as heck steps that your baby takes on their own.

You cheered so loudly.

You clapped and laughed.

You might have cried a little too.

This is the end of an era - the end of a slower-paced life, and the start of a new, faster one.

This is the start of the toddler era.

LETTER #54

FOR YOU, WHEN YOU FIND YOURSELF STARING AT THEM WHILE THEY SLEEP

Dear Mama,

Did you know something could be so beautiful?

Did you know you could stare at something for so long, and never want to stop?

Did you know you could love someone so much?

Now you know.

Now, you've felt it.

As you watch your baby sleep, their face soft and their hair messy, you've felt the beautiful blessing of motherhood.

This is our reward.

This is the reason we keep going, day after day, when our energy buckets are empty, our sleep reservoirs are dry, and we aren't sure if we can handle one more hour.

This is why.

This is love.

As you look down into their angel face while they sleep peacefully and safely, know that you are doing the sacred work of motherhood.

And you are doing it well.

LETTER #55

Dear Mama,

Let's stop the guilt-filled lies that are starting to spin through your mind.

You are not a terrible mother.

Don't let any twisted thoughts tell you otherwise.

You are human.

You make mistakes.

Every mother has yelled at her child before.

You are normal.

Motherhood is hard.

Sometimes, your patience is low and your energy is even lower.

Some days are challenging and some feel nearly impossible.

You can't be at 100% all the time.

When you find yourself yelling and feeling like the worst mother on the planet because of it, realize how very normal and human you are.

Feeling bad about how you acted is proof you are a good mother.

Wanting to do better next time is proof you are a good mother.

Trying to do things a different way next time is proof you are a good mother.

All of us mess up. Often, in fact.

But we get back up and we try again.

That is what it means to be a good mother.

LETTER #56

FOR YOU, WHEN YOUR CHILD SAYS THEIR FIRST WORD

Dear Mama,

Did you hear it??

That beautiful, purposeful sound of your baby saying their very first word...

What was it?

Was it "*mama*"?

Or "*ball*"?

Maybe it was *"hat"*.

Whatever it was - there's nothing quite like hearing your baby's voice say their very first word.

Write it down.

It doesn't matter where you write it; on a note in your phone or in their baby book - whatever you do, write it down.

And continue to write down the new words as they come...

There'll be lots of new ones now.

Celebrate their new language.

Cherish their new language.

You officially have a talker!

LETTER #57

FOR YOU, WHEN YOU BEGIN TO PLAN YOUR BABY'S FIRST BIRTHDAY

Dear Mama,

There's a saying: *"The days are long, but the years are short."* and nothing quite sums up motherhood quite like that quote.

How is it that the day of your baby's birth can feel so long ago, and also like yesterday - all at the same time?

One minute, you're holding a day-old baby in your arms as you try to figure out what you're doing.

And the next, you're looking at the calendar, making plans for your baby's first birthday.

Your baby is turning one.

One. Year. Old.

How are *you* feeling about it all?

Excited, happy...

Emotional, nostalgic...

Reminiscing about the weeks that led to delivery, and the first few weeks at home.

Thinking about all that happened this year - the first year of your baby's life.

The first year of a child's life holds so much growth and change; more than any other year.

They go from being a helpless, squirmy newborn to a little person who may even walk and talk.

All in the span of a year.

As your baby's first birthday approaches, allow yourself to feel everything.

The emotions, the memories, the hardships, the triumphs.

Soak it all in, and when the day comes - celebrate the year you've spent together.

You've both earned it.

LETTER #58

Dear Mama,

Who knew motherhood would require you to learn a
new language?

Your baby's very own special language…

By now, you are becoming fluent in the language of
your child.

You know that *"goo"* means *yogurt,* and *"mo"*
means *more.*

You know that *"hah-pee"* means *help, please,* and
"tee" means *cheese.*

Whatever your baby's language sounds like, you
know it in detail.

The funny part comes when you're around other
people, and you realize that not everyone speaks
the language of your baby.

The words your baby just spoke which make total sense to you, sound like the language of a stranger to everyone else.

It's hilarious, and also a sweet reminder of just how important and special you are to your child.

For now, you speak a language that is just yours.

Cherish it.

Also, cherish those cute pronunciations and strange words.

Write them all down.

Commit them to memory.

Not only will they make you smile in the years to come, but your child will love to hear how they used to say *strawberries* or *helicopter* when they were little.

Before long, those early pronunciations will turn into words understood by everyone who speaks the language.

But for now, revel in the sweet, hilarious pronunciations of your baby's early language.

LETTER #59

FOR YOU, WHEN YOU ANXIOUSLY LOOK FOR THE ANSWER TO YOUR LATEST PARENTING QUESTION

Dear Mama,

You are concerned, worried, and scared.

You are wondering what's normal, or if there's a problem.

You are wondering what to do, and desperately seeking information and advice.

First, take a long, deep breath.

Then repeat it a few more times.

Good job for recognizing that you have a question or a concern.

That's the first step.

The second step is to ask a trusted professional, like your child's pediatrician.

Google is a blessing but also a curse, especially for already worried parents.

Dr. Google is no match for a trusted professional that you can speak to face to face.

Lean on your resources, and find the answers to your questions.

You are doing a great job.

LETTER #60

FOR YOU, WHEN YOU LONGINGLY WONDER WHAT LIFE WAS LIKE BEFORE KIDS

Dear Mama,

Do you remember what it was like; life before kids?

Do you remember what it was like to only be responsible for yourself, and maybe a pet or two?

To eat when you're hungry, and drink your coffee while it's still hot?

To sleep in if you wanted, and watch whatever shows you felt like?

To wear one outfit for an entire day, and be able to complete your laundry in a few hours instead of a few days?

Life before kids can feel like a thousand years ago.

Life before kids can also feel like a blessed vacation when you're standing in the trenches of motherhood.

Let yourself remember what life was like before kids.

It's even ok to miss it.

It doesn't make you a bad mother to reminisce about how simple things were back then, or certainly how less exhausting they were.

They *were* easier, and you surely got more sleep.

But you know the truth deep in your bones.

Given the choice, you wouldn't go back.

You wouldn't trade this life with your little ones for sleeping in, no matter how exhausted you are.

You wouldn't trade cold leftovers and reheated coffee or spit up-stained clothes and Cocomelon for life before kids.

Because life before kids means you didn't know them.

You didn't know this piece of you; this part of your heart that actually lives outside your body.

Life before kids was quieter, calmer, and no doubt more rested.

But it didn't have them in it, and for that reason, you'll endure the exhaustion and all the laundry that comes with it.

They are worth it.

And remember this too - kids grow up and one day, you will be able to sleep 12 hours again, if you want to.

LETTER #61

FOR YOU, WHEN YOU WONDER HOW MOTHERHOOD CAN BE SO MAGICAL AND SO EXHAUSTING AT THE SAME TIME

Dear Mama,

It's the age-old paradox of motherhood.

The mystery; the cause of much mental whiplash.

How can motherhood be *so magical* and *so exhausting* at the same time??

This blessed child you are raising is a literal piece of your heart walking around outside your body.

When they hurt, you hurt.

When they are happy, you feel happy.

You feel vulnerable because you know they have the power to bring you to your knees if anything happens to them.

And seeing the world through their bright wonder-filled eyes infuses your spirit with something that evaporated after your own childhood.

Motherhood is magical.

It's a gift.

But good grief, it is exhausting.

Starting with the lack of sleep in the early days, followed by the demands of feeding a growing baby, and then engaging with and chasing after an energetic toddler.

Establishing boundaries, teaching manners, enforcing limits, and of course, keeping them healthy and safe...

It's a lot.

Especially when you don't sleep like you used to.

Being a parent has the uncanny ability to test your patience, energy levels, and chaos-tolerance in a way nothing else does.

It may seem like you're often on the losing end of that test too.

And yet... Being a mother is also one of life's biggest gifts.

Magical and exhausting.

Spectacular and depleting.

Wonderful and frustrating.

All at the very same time.

LETTER #62

FOR YOU, WHEN YOU WANT TO SKIP TO THE END OF A HARD PHASE, BUT YOU DON'T WANT TO RUSH TIME

Dear Mama,

You feel a little like you're at war with yourself, right now.

This current stage of parenting is *hard*.

Whether it's sleep regression, feeding troubles, behavioral issues, or potty training, parenting is filled with hard phases.

The war you are waging is between wanting to skip to the end of an especially hard season, to when it gets easier.

But you also know that childhood is a ticking clock.

You know your child is growing before your eyes, and every day that passes is one you'll never have again.

You know time is precious, and you don't want to rush any of the time you have with your child.

It's a tender place to be.

Acknowledge that this is a hard phase; it's ok to be frustrated and overwhelmed.

Also know that like most things, *this too shall pass*.

Time marches on and pretty soon, sleep regression or potty training will be a distant memory.

Something else will replace it.

Try your best to sit with each day, and look for whatever good you can find.

Hang on.

It will get better.

LETTER #63

FOR YOU, WHEN YOU LOOK AT OLD PHOTOS OF YOUR CHILD AND YOUR HEART PHYSICALLY HURTS

Dear Mama,

Your sweet, tender heart.

Who knew scrolling through old photos, or paging through your child's baby book could stir up so many emotions.

It's fun to remember the times that have passed; the phases your child has gone through.

Remember their favorite shirt, or the way they always put their shoes on the wrong feet?

Remember how messy they got eating yogurt, or their first time dipping their toes in the ocean?

Remember the way their eyelashes looked when they were a baby, or the chubby baby dimples on the backs of their hands?

Thank goodness for photos to help you remember exactly what each of those memories looked like.

It's a joy to look at them and reminisce.

But no one prepares you for the physical pain your heart can feel when you look at those old photos.

No one tells you about the lump that forms in your throat when you look at a photo of your child on their first birthday, and then you look at them across the room, working on their homework.

No one tells you how the swift passage of time can feel like a cruel joke to your tender heart.

Watching your child grow is a gift.

Every stage is filled with wonder, excitement, and new memories.

Raising your child is a dream come true.

But still...

The vivid reminder of how fast time is passing, and the finality of each stage's end can squeeze your heart unlike anything else.

Let yourself feel the emotions.

Give yourself grace.

Those emotions are born from love.

LETTER #64

Dear Mama,

Raising a child is filled with firsts.

First breath, first cry, first feeding, first bath.

First smile, first laugh, first word, first step.

First friend, first play date, first day of school.

So many firsts, and each new stage brings with it new firsts.

But, motherhood is filled with *lasts* too.

Last day before their umbilical cord falls off *(the last visible reminder of life inside the womb.)*

Last day wearing a smaller sized diaper, or a certain size of clothing.

Last day in a baby swing, or last day in the baby carrier.

Last night in a crib, or last time nursing.

Sometimes, you'll know when a "last" is coming. Sometimes, you can prepare for it.

But other times, the lasts are only recognized in hindsight.

Often, the lasts happen quietly, without us knowing it's going to be the last time.

How do we handle the knowledge that it's likely we'll miss some of the lasts of motherhood?

We soak up as much of the *right here, right now* that we can.

We cherish the way they look in size 2 diapers, or the way they look in their 9 month jammies.

We pay attention to the rhythmic rocking of the baby swing, or to the nursing routine.

We look closely and soak in as much of each stage as we can.

Because we know that before too long, new lasts will come and new firsts will take their place.

LETTER #65

FOR YOU, WHEN YOUR BABY HAS A FEVER

Dear Mama,

Whether it's your baby's first fever or their tenth, nothing quite squeezes your mama heart like the radiating body heat or rosy cheeks of your feverish child.

You inwardly groan and go get the thermometer.

Sure enough, they have a fever.

You didn't need the thermometer though; not really.

You can see it in their eyes.

Logically, you know a fever is a good thing - it's your child's immune response to germs.

But, when they hurt, you hurt.

When they are sad, you feel sad.

Remember that like many times before, this too shall pass.

But right now, it's stressful and it's ok to feel that way.

Sick children stir up anxiety in parents in a way that can only be understood when you're a parent yourself.

You get it.

That pit of anxiety when you look at their flushed face and sad, sick eyes.

Your baby is sick and it makes your heart hurt.

That proves you're a good mama.

For now, take a deep breath.

Go get a cold washcloth and grab the ibuprofen.

Tell yourself as many times as you need to hear it, *"It's going to be ok"*

LETTER #66

FOR YOU, WHEN YOU REALIZE YOU CAN PICK OUT YOUR BABY'S CRY IN A CROWDED ROOM

Dear Mama,

You're in a place with lots of children; a store, a playground, a friend's house.

Kids are all over, making noise and chaos.

Then you hear it.

Among all of the voices, whines, and cries, you hear it...

Your baby's cry.

It's a miraculous talent of a mother - the ability to pick the sound of her child's cry from a crowded room.

Dozens of children making noise, sometimes all at once, but when your child cries - you hear it.

They need you.

They are looking for you.

You are their safe place.

Knowing your child's cry is instinctual; it's built into the DNA of a mother.

The world around you might be filled with noise, but when your child cries, you hear it.

LETTER #67

FOR YOU, WHEN YOU FEEL REDUCED TO A MILK MACHINE

Dear Mama,

Sometimes, your entire existence as a mother can feel reduced to two words: *milk machine.*

Or if we're really being honest, sometimes you just feel like a cow. *A dairy cow.*

Feeding, burping, diapering, and then feeding again.

Pumping, feeding, pumping, feeding.

You get the overwhelming feeling that the only thing you are doing is producing milk and feeding it to your baby.

And sometimes, you're not wrong.

But here's the truth - you are a miraculous human.

Your body is producing milk that can fully sustain a human baby for months, giving them every single thing they need to grow from a teeny newborn to a baby that's capable of crawling.

You grew your baby inside your body, and now you are sustaining them with milk from your body too...

It's completely exhausting.

It's often uncomfortable.

And sometimes, it's just plain annoying.

But wow, is it ever miraculous!

There are times when you will feel like the equivalent of a dairy cow.

This is never as true as when you're hooked up to a breast pump, with the rhythmic suction humming and milk collecting in containers as you watch it pass through the tubing.

It's ok... You can be annoyed, and you definitely can laugh.

But let yourself be amazed too.

Let yourself be proud of the milk your body is producing, the milk you are collecting with that pump, and the milk you are feeding your baby.

You really are incredible.

LETTER #68

FOR YOU, WHEN YOUR BRAIN FEELS MUSHY AND YOU CAN'T REMEMBER WHAT YOU USED TO BE LIKE BEFORE KIDS

Dear Mama,

When you haven't showered in days, and haven't slept in even longer, your brain tends to get a little mushy.

Your sweats have stains you can't identify, and you don't remember if you've even eaten today.

You're not sure what day it is, and suddenly, you realize you haven't left the house in at least a week.

This is often one of those times when you find yourself forgetting what you were like before you became a mother.

It feels so long ago...

When you only had to feed yourself.

When you only had to clothe yourself.

When you only had to bathe yourself.

Of course your mind was clearer and sharper then!

You were focused only on taking care of yourself.

It's ok to feel jealous of your former self.

It's ok to wistfully imagine what it would be like to only care for yourself for a whole entire day.

It's ok to lament your foggy, mushy brain and your stained sweatpants.

But this isn't how you're going to be forever.

This isn't how you're going to feel forever.

Your child will grow older.

Your season of life will evolve and change.

Your clothes will stay cleaner and you will get more sleep.

Your brain will shake the cobwebs out and you'll see things a little clearer.

One day, the fog of the early years will lift and you'll find yourself in a new phase of life.

For now, miss your former self, and be kind to your current self.

You are doing the best you can.

LETTER #69

FOR YOU, WHEN YOU TAKE THE FAMILY PICTURES BUT ARE NEVER IN ANY

Dear Mama,

You are the photographer in your family.

Your camera roll is filled with photos from the big and small moments of life.

Your child dressed up for Christmas, or smiling proudly on their birthday.

Sleepy eyes and tousled bed head on a Saturday morning, and messy faces after ice cream treats on summer nights.

You capture the moments of their life, both big and small, so you can look back on them later.

Maybe you make photo books with the photos, or you print them and put them into a baby book.

However you preserve the memories, your camera roll is filled with proof of your life together.

But here's the thing...

If you look closely, how many photos are *you* actually in?

Not very many.

You are always the one taking the photos, so you aren't in them very often.

That needs to change.

You need to get in the photos too.

Start with selfies.

Next, utilize your phone's 10 second self-timer.

Prop your phone up, set the timer, and get in position.

Take photos with yourself in them, no matter what you look like that day.

No more excuses.

Your children deserve to have photos with their mother in them too.

They will be forever grateful.

LETTER #70

Dear Mama,

No one prepares you for it.

No one tells you how it will stop you in your tracks and take your breath away.

But it will.

You won't know when it will happen.

Maybe you'll be giving your child a bath, or maybe they'll be proudly showing you a new art project or a new athletic trick.

You could be tucking them into bed at night, or watching them walk out of their room in the morning with sleepy eyes and rumpled bed head.

You won't know when it's going to happen but sooner or later, it will.

All of a sudden, you will look at your child and for just a second, you'll see what they will be like when they are 18.

You'll see them as a teenager.

You'll see them as they are becoming an adult.

Just for a second, they won't be the little child in front of you - they will be a nearly grown adult, in the place where your baby used to be.

When it happens, your chest might get tight.

Your eyes might widen.

And you surely will swallow a lump in your throat.

That bittersweet glimpse reminds you of the swift passage of time, and the reality that your child gets older every single day.

Watching them get older is a gift.

But for your tender mama heart, it's also bittersweet as you say goodbye to each passing stage and year.

Let this glimpse into the future be a teacher.

Let it remind you to pay attention now.

Let the flash of your child at 18 years old help you to watch closely now, and memorize how they are, *today*.

You can't stop the passage of time.

And you probably wouldn't, even if you could.

But you *can* slow it down by truly paying attention and cherishing them as they are, right now.

LETTER #71

FOR YOU, WHEN YOU REALIZE YOU JUST ACTED EXACTLY AS YOUR PARENTS USED TO

Dear Mama,

Like most, your youth was probably filled with times you swore you'd be different than your parents when you grew up.

Even if your childhood was wonderful and happy, there were times you didn't like the rules or the routines, and you promised you would do things differently when it was your turn.

Now, it's your turn.

Now, you have your own family.

And still... the time will come when you do something or say something and you'll realize you're doing it *exactly* like your own parents did.

You'll realize they actually knew what they were doing after all.

It's humbling... and wonderful.

Because now you really know and understand how challenging parenthood can be.

You understand how much your parents loved you, because you know how much you love your child.

Now, you know what it's like on the other side, and you know everything they did came from a place of love.

Everything they did comes from the same place you parent your own child from, now.

It comes from love.

LETTER #72

Dear Mama,

You had a plan.

You had a plan for birth, a plan for breastfeeding, a plan for sleep training, and a plan for potty training.

And probably a plan for everything else from kid-friendly travel to kindergarten placement.

Sometimes, those plans work great.

Things go smoothly and everything works out like you hoped it would.

But not always.

Sometimes, things don't go as planned.

Sometimes, circumstances change, things happen, and you have to change course.

Those times can leave you wondering and worrying if your child will turn out alright.

Will they be ok?

Will this setback, this change of plan cause lasting impacts on their life?

The future is unknown, but please know this.

You are doing the very best you can.

You are doing the best you can for yourself and for your child.

You are there for them, no matter what.

And most likely, everything is going to work out just fine.

LETTER #73

Dear Mama,

The decisions in parenthood start early.

Find out the gender? Share the baby's name?
Natural delivery or epidural? Breastfeed or bottle
feed?

Sometimes, they're as casual as what color to paint
the nursery walls, or whether to buy gender-neutral
onesies.

But other times, they are bigger decisions like how
and when to introduce solid foods, or your
preferred sleep training methods.

As your child grows, the decisions will continue,
and will have even bigger impacts on their life.

What activities will they participate in?

Where will they go to school?

Each decision can feel overwhelming, with too
many options to choose from.

Each decision can feel monumental, regardless of its true size and impact.

As you find yourself agonizing over the decisions you have to make for your child, find refuge in this truth...

If there was a true *"best"* choice, you would know it, and you would choose it.

If you aren't sure what choice is better, and you're going back and forth between options, in the long run it probably doesn't matter what you pick.

If you're waffling back and forth between two choices, in the grand scheme of things, your child will probably be fine no matter what you choose.

The decisions may still feel overwhelming.

But know that the lifelong impact of your choice is probably not going to cause harm.

Make your decisions with thought and care.

But don't let them overwhelm and overtake you.

Don't let yourself agonize and despair over decisions that probably won't matter either way in the long run.

Unless there's a very clear right or wrong choice, give yourself some grace.

Think about it, talk about it, pray about it... and then pick one.

If it doesn't work out, pick something new.

Give yourself permission to make a decision and go with it, and pivot if needed.

LETTER #74

FOR YOU, WHEN YOU FEEL BURDENED WITH MOM GUILT

Dear Mama,

"Mom guilt" is when you feel guilty for well... anything related to motherhood.

Maybe you feel guilty because you have to go back to work, and you feel guilty for putting your child in daycare.

Maybe you feel guilty for buying pre-made baby food, instead of making your own.

Maybe you feel guilty for using disposable diapers instead of cloth diapers, or for putting your baby in their crib instead of co-sleeping *(or vice versa.)*

Maybe you feel guilty because you didn't host an elaborate birthday party for your child, or didn't bring treats to their classroom for their birthday.

Maybe you feel guilty because you just yelled at your child, or locked yourself in the bathroom for a few minutes of peace.

Guilt wraps you in feelings of *defeat, failure,* and *shame.*

Mama, you are not alone.

We all feel the mom guilt.

We all wish we didn't, but we do.

Each one of us is simply doing the very best we can.

Each one of us is trying to raise our babies the best we know how, and the best we have the capacity for.

Some of us want to work and some of us want to stay home.

Some of us want to make baby food, and others want to buy it at Target.

Some of us want to co-sleep or use cloth diapers, and others want to use a crib or disposable diapers.

Instead of feeling guilty over our choices, we should be saying *"who cares?!"* and offering a big high five to ourselves and each other.

We are raising children!

We are keeping little humans alive every day!

We are juggling motherhood with all of the other expectations on our shoulders, and we are doing the best we can.

Mom guilt is not helpful.

Mom guilt is not kind.

Mom guilt is not useful.

If you are burdened and weary with mom guilt, you are not alone.

You don't have anything to be guilty about.

You are doing the best you can, and for that, you should be celebrated.

LETTER #75

FOR YOU, WHEN YOU ARE FORCED TO ACCEPT CHANGED PLANS

Dear Mama,

Sometimes things don't work out like you hoped, and you are forced to accept the outcome.

Usually, this is out of your control.

Maybe you wanted a natural delivery, and instead required a c-section for the safety of your baby or yourself.

Maybe you wanted to breastfeed for a year, and because of reasons out of your control, you had to stop and switch to formula.

Maybe you wanted to stay home with your baby, but instead had to return to work and place your baby in childcare.

When plans change and things you hoped for end, allow yourself to grieve.

Endings are usually bittersweet.

Endings are especially hard when you don't choose them.

Whether that ending is the end of a plan, the end of a dream, or the end of a motherhood phase like breastfeeding, it can feel especially sad and traumatic when you didn't choose it.

Grieve the loss of the plan, dream, or phase.

Grieve the loss of what you hoped to experience.

Let yourself feel the sadness, frustration, and anger.

It's ok to feel all of it.

You are strong, and resilient.

You are going to be ok.

LETTER #76

FOR YOU, WHEN YOU FEEL CAUGHT BETWEEN THE SHOULDS AND SHOULDN'TS IN MOTHERHOOD

Dear Mama,

Motherhood is overwhelming.

It has probably always been overwhelming, but it's especially so in the modern digital era.

Not only do we have countless options of gadgets, gear, and methods of parenting, but now, we also have access to billions of people's lives and opinions at our fingertips.

The number of options can feel paralyzing.

The flood of opinions can feel suffocating.

The shoulds and shouldn'ts can threaten to overwhelm you and cause you to doubt every single decision you make.

Should you deliver at home or at a hospital?

Should you get an epidural or not?

Should you have a repeat c-section or a VBAC?

Should you breastfeed or bottle feed?

What breast pump is the best?

What baby carrier is the best?

The questions are innumerable, and the opinions and advice from people come faster than you can absorb, especially on the internet.

It's no wonder modern mothers are overwhelmed and stressed in a way that's never been experienced by any generation before.

When you feel caught in the middle of the shoulds and shouldn'ts, the first thing to do is silence the noise.

Go offline for a while.

Unplug.

Quiet the noise and give yourself space to listen to your own heart.

If you need guidance, ask people who really know you.

If you need help from a professional, find one and ask.

Don't let Dr. Google or people on Facebook give you advice you should only get from your OB or your child's pediatrician.

For many of the questions that threaten to overwhelm the modern mother, there is no *right* or *wrong* answer.

Baby carriers come in hundreds of different styles, brands, colors, and functionalities for a reason.

What works for someone else might not be best for you.

And honestly, who cares which one you use?!

As long as it works for you and doesn't cause any harm, you're good.

The same holds true for the rest of decisions in motherhood; diapers, clothing colors, baby food, sleeping arrangements, car seat brands, sleep training… and the list continues.

When the noise threatens to overwhelm you and makes you second-guess every decision you make, take it as a sign to stop and unplug.

Sign offline and quiet the noise.

Listen to yourself and the trusted people in your life.

That's where you will find the best answers to your motherhood questions.

LETTER #77

Dear Mama,

It happened again... you rolled over in the middle of the night and there's a little body in your bed.

Or maybe you were pulled from your sleep with a hushed whisper, *"Mamaaaa..."*

It might be because of a bad dream, a storm, a scary monster or simply because they missed you.

Your child is in bed with you... again.

It's your choice how to handle it.

If your sleep is suffering and it's impacting how you handle your days, it's ok to be firm in your boundaries.

It's ok to have limits, and to enforce them.

Let them lay with you for a few minutes and walk them back to their bed.

Let them know your bed is your space and you need sleep just like they do.

It's ok to make them go back to their bed.

On the flip side, no teenager is going to want to sleep in bed with their parents.

So, if you like having your child in bed with you, let them stay.

If you can sleep with them in bed, cherish the closeness.

Cherish the sleepy warmth.

Cherish the memory.

It'll be over before you know it.

Remember, it's ok to prioritize your own sleep.

It's ok to be supportive but also firm with your boundaries.

And, if they really need to be close, compromise by laying a pillow and blanket on the floor by your bed.

LETTER #78

FOR YOU, WHEN YOU WONDER IF IT'S TIME TO POTTY TRAIN

Dear Mama,

Like so many things with parenting, there are dozens of different thoughts, views, and methods surrounding potty training.

Some people advocate simple modeling; letting your child learn from you when they're ready.

Some people promote a 3-day potty training boot camp, and swear by it.

Others try something in the middle, or one of the many other options.

It can feel completely overwhelming to approach the potty training milestone, especially for the very first time.

It's scary, it's strange, and you've likely heard so many horror stories.

Before you start asking for opinions or advice, or making potty training plans, please know this...

Your child *will* be potty trained someday.

Whether it happens next month or a year from now, they won't be wearing diapers in elementary school.

Also, every child is different.

What worked for one friend or in one book may not work best for you.

Research the options, and ask for advice.

Make a plan if you want to try it.

But hold it all loosely... Things may go differently than you planned.

Above all, know that *you* have to be ready before you dive into potty training your child.

You have to be ready for all of the changes that come when you trade diapers for underwear.

Frequent trips to the bathroom in the middle of running errands, extra changes of clothes in the diaper bag and every vehicle, and ample patience for the process.

If you aren't mentally prepared, wait a while.

If you aren't mentally ready for what potty training requires of you, give yourself a little more time.

And when you and your child are ready, go for it.

It might even be easier than you think.

Letter #79

Dear Mama,

Your child is getting a new bed.

You're getting ready to say goodbye to the crib as you make space for something new.

Many of the "lasts" in parenting are only recognized in hindsight; you don't know it's the last time until the moment is gone.

But this time... you know the end of an era is coming.

You know this will be your baby's last night in their crib.

Change is exciting but it is also bittersweet.

Removing the crib from your child's room is a statement of growth; a shift from baby to toddler.

Your child is growing up.

As you prepare to lay your child down to sleep for the last night in their crib, take a minute and look around.

Soak up what their room looks like with the crib in it.

Take a few pictures.

Memorize what they look like as they lay in their crib - where they've slept since they were born.

This is the end of an era; one of the "lasts" of parenthood.

But this time, you know it's coming.

This time, you can pay attention and appreciate this milestone.

And then, you can celebrate that awesome new bed.

LETTER #80

FOR YOU, WHEN YOU HIT YOUR WALL WITH SLEEP DEPRIVATION

Dear Mama,

How long has it been since you've slept more than a few hours in a row?

Can you even remember?

Maybe it's been months, or maybe it's even been years.

Maybe you can't remember the last time you slept more than two hours in a row, without being woken up.

And you are tired.

The kind of tired that seeps deep into your bones, and dulls all of your senses.

The kind of tired a nap or one miraculous 4 hour stretch at night can't fix.

When you have been severely sleep deprived for so long, there comes a time when you simply can't do it anymore.

You hit your wall.

This is the time to call in reinforcements.

Did you know there are sleep consultants for babies?

A person you can hire to help you sleep train your baby.

Someone who can virtually hold your hand and tell you what to do to get your baby *(and you)* sleeping again.

Google it.

Hire one if you possibly can.

You'll know it when you hit your wall of sleep deprivation.

When you simply don't have the stamina to endure the lack of sleep any longer.

Turn to those who can help you.

It works miracles.

They will help you sleep again.

Letter #81

For you, when you consider trying for another baby

Dear Mama,

Your baby is not so little anymore, and your body has recovered from delivery.

The haze of the newborn days has lifted, and you begin to wonder.

Or maybe you already know.

You want to have another baby.

But when is the right time to start trying?

Take a look at your life and the immediate future.

Are there any major hurdles coming that would make waiting a smart choice?

Or do you feel nervously ready right now?

You can do your best to plan, and with a decision this big, you should.

But as you well know, plans change and things don't always work out like you thought they would.

Either way, take a deep breath.

Consider your heart; what is it telling you?

Just like when deciding to try to get pregnant the first time, you might not feel completely "ready" yet.

But pregnancy takes 9 months for a reason.

It might feel scary to think about doing it all over again.

It might feel sad that your baby won't be your only focus anymore.

But it might also feel exciting too - you've dreamed of a sibling for your child, and this next step will get you there.

Consider your heart, and you'll know what to do.

And in the meantime, shower your firstborn with all of the love and attention you can muster.

LETTER #82

FOR YOU, WHEN YOU WORRY ABOUT LOVING YOUR SECOND CHILD AS MUCH AS YOUR FIRST

Dear Mama,

You have entered new territory - growing a baby on the inside while parenting another on the outside.

Caring for a child while going through pregnancy is no easy feat, no matter how hard or easy pregnancy is for you.

It can be a lot.

Your heart is undoubtedly happy, excited, and anxious.

And maybe even a little bit uncertain.

As you look at your firstborn child, you might wonder if it's possible to love anyone else as much as you love them.

Will you be able to love your second child as much as you love your first?

It's a question that's been asked by mothers for ages.

And as every mother who has more than one child will assure you, the answer is yes - you will love your second as much as your first.

Love is not a finite thing; it is not a pie to be divided.

If it were a pie, your firstborn would start with the whole thing, but then have to split your love with their new sibling.

Thankfully, love doesn't work like that.

Your heart is capable of infinite love.

It's a magical mystery, impossible to explain or describe.

But that doesn't mean it's not true.

You won't know for sure until it happens to you.

But trust the billions of mothers who have gone before you.

Trust that love will expand.

You can love your second baby as much as your first.

And you will.

LETTER #83

FOR YOU, WHEN YOU WATCH YOUR CHILDREN PLAY TOGETHER

Dear Mama,

Having a second child brings a whole new level of joy to a family.

You get to watch your firstborn become a sibling.

You get to see them learn to love the new baby.

You get to see them be a helper, and do what they can to interact and care for their new brother or sister.

It's precious and it's sweet.

But nothing compares to the joy that fills your heart when your children begin to play together; as in truly, intentionally, play together.

Interacting, imagining, encouraging each other.

Watching your children play together is a vivid reminder of the gift you gave each one of them - *a sibling.*

Watch them play.

Enjoy it.

Cherish it.

This is what siblings are made for.

LETTER #84

FOR YOU, WHEN YOUR KIDS
FIGHT SO LOUD YOU THINK
YOUR EARDRUMS MIGHT BURST

Dear Mama,

How can siblings play happily one minute, and the next, they are screaming at each other at the top of their lungs?

How can moods and attitudes change so fast?

It's mind-boggling to a parent, but is it ever true!

You notice your kids playing nicely and quietly together, and the clock starts ticking...

How long until one of them comes crying?

How long until one of them tattles on the other?

How long until they are fighting so loudly, you wish you had earplugs?

Parenting two *(or more)* kids is a remarkable test of patience.

It's also a marvelous study of how fast anger can flare up, and then diffuse, and pass.

166

Your children can go from playing to fighting, and back to playing faster than it takes to pop a bag of popcorn in the microwave.

How???

Soak up the times they play nicely together.

Enjoy the peace and quiet when they're happily on the same page.

And be ready when the tide turns and they come running.

Also, if needed, invest in a pair of quality ear plugs.

LETTER #85

Dear Mama,

Being a mother has always been hard.

Each era of motherhood saw its own set of challenges, and all of them shared some of the same ones too.

But this one?

Being a mother in the digital age?

It's a brand new beast, and it's a big one.

Never before in the history of motherhood were there so many opinions, products, theories, methods and outcomes as mothers face right now.

The internet and social media in particular have changed *everything.*

Previous generations of mothers asked trusted family and friends for advice and usually did what they did.

Now, mothers have the entire world at their fingertips, as well as the overwhelm that comes with it.

The options in parenting are endless.

Breastfeeding or bottle? Crib or family bed? Gentle parenting or firm discipline? Sleep training? Organic? Homeschool? Screen time? Artificial dyes?

The sheer number of things to care about, and choices to make is overwhelming.

Then, add in the number of different opinions on social media, with the vehement attitude that everyone's way is the only right way.

What happens if you're doing it differently?

Suddenly, you are doing it wrong... or it sure feels that way.

One post, one picture on social media has the power to make you feel like you're doing everything wrong.

One comment from a stranger can make you feel like a failure.

But only if you let it.

The truth is, there are millions of different ways to parent a child.

There are millions of different products you can use, and even more opinions surrounding them.

But no one is *you,* and no one is parenting *your child.*

You are in charge of your life.

You are in charge of your baby.

Everyone else has an opinion about everything, but you don't have to ask for it.

You don't have to listen to it.

And you sure don't have to let it affect your perception of how you are as a mother.

If you see something on social media that makes you feel like a failure, close the app.

If you keep seeing things that make you feel like you're doing everything wrong, delete the app.

Seek insight, counsel, and help from trusted family, friends, and the true medical professionals in your life.

The army of opinions, choices, and motives on social media does *not* get to make you feel like a failure.

Not anymore.

LETTER #86

FOR YOU, WHEN YOUR CHILD
FINDS THEIR FIRST HOBBY

Dear Mama,

Watching your child grow up is fun.

Bittersweet, of course; sometimes, it's emotionally overwhelming and just plain sad.

But it's also joyful and entertaining.

Watching your kid find their first hobby?

Now that's exciting.

Maybe it's superheroes, stuffed animals, dinosaurs, or construction trucks.

Maybe it's rocks, ballet, swimming, or playing trains.

Whatever your child's first hobby is, watching them develop an intentional interest in something is amazing.

Celebrate that hobby with them.

Nurture that interest as much as you can.

Foster a love of going all in when something grabs their attention.

Developing hobbies is a skill they will carry with them for life.

LETTER #87

FOR YOU, WHEN YOU ARE
WORRIED ABOUT SCREEN TIME

Dear Mama,

You've heard the warnings about screen time.

The data from the experts and the recommendations that all come from a good-hearted place.

They mean well, and there is truth to their stance.

But their recommendations can also cause worry, guilt, and shame if we aren't careful.

If you want to follow the guidelines to a T and you are able to, go for it.

You do you.

But limiting or banning screen time doesn't make you a superior parent.

If you want to use screen time as part of your parenting tools, go for it.

Using screen time doesn't make you an inferior parent.

Here's the truth - screen time is a tool, with the power to be used for good or bad.

Unlimited, constant screen time that gets in the way of children exercising their imagination, challenging their brains, and most of all, playing outside?

No one can argue that's a good idea.

Of course that's the *wrong* way to use screen time.

But intermittent, well-monitored screen time, controlled by a parent, and used as a tool with boundaries to facilitate a smooth family routine?

That is screen time as a helpful, positive parenting tool.

Don't let the experts' blanket recommendations cause you guilt and shame.

Their recommendations are primarily made to protect from screen time's negative extremes.

And for good reason.

Their recommendations aren't made to shame you from using PBS Kids as a tool to keep your kids occupied while you cook dinner or finish up a work project in peace.

Like most things in parenting, you get to be the judge of what works for you.

You are the one who decides how much or how little screen time works for you and your family.

You are the only one who knows what is necessary for a smooth morning routine, or a smooth evening routine.

You are the only one who knows your children, and who knows your energy levels.

Screen time is a tool, just like anything else.

Use it smartly, and you have nothing to feel guilty about.

No matter what anyone or any organization says to the contrary.

LETTER #88

FOR YOU, WHEN YOU FEEL BAD BECAUSE YOUR KID ATE FAST FOOD... AGAIN

Dear Mama,

The guilt arrives as you pull into the parking lot, and grows as you give your order.

By the time you get to the window to pay, you're feeling the full-blown onslaught of guilt.

Your child is eating fast food... again.

Maybe it's McDonalds, maybe it's Arby's or something different all together.

But the guilt is the same.

We've been taught that fast food is bad, and sure, it's not the healthiest option out there.

But here's the thing - just like with babies, with children - *fed is best.*

Sometimes, you're so busy, you don't have time to make a meal.

Sometimes, you're so tired, you don't have the energy to make a meal.

Sometimes, your child earns a reward and their prize of choice is a Happy Meal.

Whatever the reason you're pulling into the drive thru again, know this.

Soon, your child is going to have a full belly.

Soon, your child is going to have their thirst quenched.

Soon, your child is going to be happily playing with their plastic toy - even if it's just for five minutes.

Right now, you are getting your child fed and that's a win.

Life won't always be this busy, and you won't always be this tired.

Maybe tomorrow, you can stick a few extra veggies in their lunchbox or on their dinner plate.

But right now, you are getting your child fed, and that only means one thing.

You are a good mom, and you're doing a great job.

LETTER #89

FOR YOU, WHEN YOU CAN'T GET YOUR CHILD TO EAT A VEGETABLE

Dear Mama,

You keep trying, you keep offering, and you keep adding them to the edge of their plate.

You model eating them, and you give a choice of dipping sauce.

But it doesn't matter what you try, the results are always the same.

The vegetables end up left on the plate, slid onto the floor, or you engage in a battle of wills, forcing every bite of vegetable into your disgusted child's mouth.

What happened to the little baby that willingly ate mushy peas and sweet potatoes?

What happened to the little toddler who worked on their pincer grasp with bite-sized pieces of beans and cooked carrots?

When did vegetables become the enemy?

The truth is, kids grow.

Opinions change.

And very often, vegetables become one of the most rejected foods of young children.

Sure, there are some kids who eat veggies willingly, and their parents are either incredibly grateful, or they naively think their child is typical.

But really, the vegetable-loving kids are the rare ones.

Most children may eat a carrot or two, or take a bite of broccoli but they do it with ulterior motives *(dessert.)*

This is normal.

Your child isn't an anomaly.

Most of all, this is not a sign of your parenting failure, as much as it might feel that way.

Children are notoriously picky eaters, and they'll likely stay that way for a while.

All you can do is continue to offer, encourage, and model eating vegetables.

Chances are, as they grow, they'll develop an appreciation for some of them; maybe even most of them.

But right now?

Stay calm, keep offering, and go buy a quality gummy vitamin to bridge the nutrient gap.

LETTER #90

FOR YOU, WHEN YOU WANT TO RESCUE THEM

Dear Mama,

Watching your child struggle is hard.

Maybe it's climbing the ladder at the playground, or learning to ride a bike.

Or maybe it's learning how to write their name, or do a three-digit addition problem.

Whatever the situation, it's hard to watch your child fight to do something.

It's hard to watch them struggle.

It's hard to watch them suffer.

But you know you can't always rescue your child; not right away anyway.

When they aren't in actual danger, and when you're available if needed, it's ok for your child to work for a solution to their problem.

It's ok for you to grit your teeth, and ball your hands into fists to keep from interfering.

It's good for your child to wrestle with it, and work it out on their own.

This makes them proud.

This builds their confidence.

This is how they grow.

It's hard to watch your child struggle while you silently stand by and watch.

But, you are helping them stretch their wings.

You are helping them become who they are meant to be.

You are doing all of this as you wait on the edge, silently ready to step in if they need it.

And when they do it themselves?

You celebrate their victory with them.

LETTER #91

FOR YOU, WHEN THEY RUN TO YOU WHEN THEY'RE HURT

Dear Mama,

You are their safe place.

You are their refuge.

You are their *fix-it;* their *make-it-better.*

That's why they come crying when they fall down.

That's why they run to you when they are hurt

That's why the first thing they do when they are sad, embarrassed, or injured is look around to find you.

When they spot you, they come to you.

It's as if gravity pulls them to you.

Actually, it's comfort, safety, and a mother's love.

When you open your arms wide and kneel down as they come to you, you are showing them they belong there.

You are showing them you are ready for their vulnerability, their emotions, and their pain.

You are showing them you are their home, and they are safe.

LETTER #92

FOR YOU, WHEN YOU NEED A MAMA FRIEND

Dear Mama,

Sometimes, you just need a mama friend.

Someone who understands how amazing and exhausting being a mother is.

Someone like you, who gives so much of themselves that it can almost feel like they are disappearing.

Someone who knows what it's like to be near the end of your rope when you haven't slept in days, and the kids just won't stop fighting.

Sometimes, you just need someone who is going through it too; someone who truly gets it.

Someone who can nod with empathy, and tell you you're doing a good job.

When it feels like you are failing, and screwing everything up, you need a mama friend to tell you the truth…

That you are doing the hardest job on the planet, and you are succeeding every day.

Your children are fed.

Your children are clothed.

Your children are safe, happy, and loved.

You need a friend to speak this truth to your weary soul and remind you that motherhood is hard.

But you are doing a great job.

And you can tell her the same thing, because she needs to hear it too.

LETTER #93

FOR YOU, WHEN YOU JUST NEED YOUR MOM

Dear Mama,

Once in a while, you just need your mom.

It doesn't matter how old you are, how many kids you have, or how far away your mom lives.

Despite the fact that you are someone else's mom now, every now and then, you just need your mom.

Sometimes, you just need the comfort, love, and kind words of the first woman who loved you.

Sometimes, you just need to be told everything is going to be ok, and reassured that you'll be fine, like she did so many times in your life before this.

Sometimes, you just need to pretend you are a child again, and your mom is capable of fixing everything, the way you do for your own kids.

It doesn't matter how old you are, how much has happened in your life, or even how old your children are, sometimes, you just need your mom.

If you can, go see her.

If you can, go talk to her.

If you can, go hug her.

Let her love wrap you up and soothe your weary soul.

And if she's in heaven already, feel the longing, feel the grief of missing her.

But know that you can still talk to her; and pay attention, because you might be surprised by the answers

Because no matter what, sooner or later, we all just need our mom.

LETTER #94

FOR YOU, WHEN YOU WONDER
IF YOU'RE DOING THINGS RIGHT

Dear Mama,

Much of motherhood has an underlying worry running through it... whether or not you are doing things right.

Are you making the right choices?

Are you doing the right things?

Are you giving your child all they need to thrive?

Are you doing enough?

Are *you* enough?

These questions and the uneasiness they cause hums beneath the surface of our daily lives as mothers.

We love these little humans with our whole heart and soul - of course we want to do the very best we can for them.

But in a world this huge, with this many different ways of doing things, and this many conflicting opinions, how do we know what's right?

How do we know if we are doing enough?

How do we know if we are good mothers?

Here's the first clue... the fact you are even asking the question proves you are a good mother.

The fact you care so deeply and want to be the best mother possible proves you love and adore them.

It proves you are a good mother.

Secondly, the only way to keep the doubts and worries at bay is to focus on your child.

Are they safe, happy, fed, clothed, and loved?

Yes?

Then you are doing a wonderful job.

It's as simple as that.

LETTER #95

FOR YOU, WHEN YOU SECOND-GUESS YOURSELF

Dear Mama,

Sometimes, it's hard to trust yourself.

Especially if this is your first baby, but even if it's not; it's easy to second-guess yourself and the choices you make.

With millions of options for parenting, it can feel impossible to trust yourself.

To trust your opinions.

To trust you are making the right choices.

It's easy, and normal, to second-guess yourself.

You are human, after all.

Here's the truth... you are doing the very best you can.

You are making decisions with deliberation, careful thought, and most of all - love for your child.

You are doing everything in your power to provide a calm, happy, loving environment for them to grow up in, and you are succeeding at that every day.

You are doing this in the middle of the most volatile, fast-moving culture Earth has ever seen.

This digital age we live in is unlike anything humanity has ever experienced before, and with it comes a whole slew of new challenges that previous generations of parents didn't have to deal with.

You are walking in uncharted territory.

We all are.

And all of us are doing the best we can, with what we have, when we have it.

You are doing the best you can, and you are doing a great job.

LETTER #96

FOR YOU, WHEN YOU JUST WANT TO SLEEP FOR A WEEK

Dear Mama,

Sleep... How can a simple five-letter word be so significant?

One of the hallmarks of parenthood is the changes it brings to your sleep habits.

Often only appreciated in hindsight, all of us took our ability to get a full night's sleep for granted before we became parents.

It's only when you can't sleep a full night anymore than you realize how luxurious and precious it was.

But once that baby is born, sleep becomes disrupted, inconsistent, and often not even close to being truly restful.

Sleep is sacrificed in the early days of raising children.

At first, the sleep deprivation might not seem so bad, but after a while, it builds.

The exhaustion grows until one day, you feel it deep in your bones.

Your brain moves slower, and you feel as if you're experiencing life through a hazy fog.

Sleep becomes something you dream about, fantasize about, and long for.

Sometimes, you swear you could sleep for a week if you had the opportunity.

The yearning for sleep can be so deep, so visceral, that you cry just thinking about it.

We've all been there.

Take heart - it will not always be like this.

You won't always be overcome with an exhaustion that makes it hard to function.

You *will* sleep again one day.

But right now, *"one day"* isn't much of a consolation to you and your truly exhausted self.

If you can, take a nap today, even if it's just for 20 minutes.

Give yourself the gift of rest, as much or as little as you can.

Call in reinforcements, and have someone watch your child while you rest.

If you need to, Google "baby sleep consultants."

Do whatever you need to help you get through today.

And know that one day, you *will* sleep again, no matter how far away it seems.

LETTER #97

Dear Mama,

On one hand, it feels like you've been a mother forever.

But on the other hand, it seems like just yesterday you were in labor and your child was born.

The way it can feel so long ago and just like yesterday is one of the great mysteries of parenthood.

You were with them through the newborn days, and the baby stages.

Then came the toddler years, and the early child years.

And now?

You are filling out forms, buying a backpack, and filling it with school supplies.

You are buying a lunchbox, and maybe even mapping out a bus route.

You are meeting teachers and walking through school buildings.

It's time for your child to go to Kindergarten.

How did you get here?

Time passed so fast.

Bittersweet emotions swirl. You are so excited for them and this new adventure.

And you're excited for yourself too; this means more time for you.

But it also means closing the door to the baby years.

It's the end of an era.

It's a major life transition.

As you help them get dressed and put on their shoes, as you take those First Day of Kindergarten photos, give yourself grace.

Swallow the lump in your throat and blink through the tears that are blurring your eyes.

It's bittersweet and emotional, and it's ok to feel all of the emotions at once.

Your baby is growing up.

And you get a front row seat to watch it happen.

What a gift that is.

A priceless, emotional, bittersweet gift.

One last hug, wave goodbye, and allow yourself to feel everything.

At the end of the day, be ready with arms wide open to welcome them back home again.

Your baby is in Kindergarten now.

LETTER #98

Dear Mama,

They've held your hand hundreds or maybe even thousands of times before.

You've felt their hand in yours, sure... but have you really stopped to pay attention to what it feels like?

The way their little hand slips up into yours.

The warmth of their soft skin.

The squishy, dimpled knuckles of the back of their hand.

The squeeze they give your hand as it wraps around theirs.

Stop for a second and really feel it.

Pay attention.

Soak in everything about it.

One day, their dimpled knuckles will disappear, and they won't reach for your hand anymore.

One day, this will be a distant memory.

But that day is not today.

Today, you can memorize what it's like to hold your child's hand.

Today, you can hold it a little longer, and squeeze it a little tighter.

Today, you can pay attention, and appreciate what a gift this really is.

LETTER #99

FOR YOU, WHEN YOU REALLY
STOP AND LOOK AT THEM

Dear Mama,

Life is busy and you feel pulled in many different directions.

You're moving from breakfast to school, to pickup and sports, to supper and bedtime, only to have it start all over again the next day.

Or maybe you haven't moved past the early baby years yet, and your days are an endless loop of feedings, diaper changes, naps, and laundry.

Either way, life feels like it passes by in a blur, punctuated by milestones like birthdays or holidays.

Today, take a moment to stop and really look at your child.

Notice what you see.

Look at the way their hair falls around their face, and grazes the back of their neck.

Look at the way their eyelashes curl, and the striking color of their eyes.

Look at the soft skin of their face, and the plump lips that seem to be often curved into a smile.

Look at their dimpled knuckles, or at their slender hands where the dimples used to be.

Look at their face's profile - the same profile you stared at in an ultrasound picture.

Stop and pay attention to everything about them.

Listen to their voice.

Listen to the way they pronounce their words.

Listen to their giggles, and the way their belly laughs sound.

Even listen to the sounds they make when they whine or cry...

Soak up every detail you can about them, just as they are right now.

Every day, they get a little bit older.

Every day, they change just a little bit.

It's so subtle day-to-day, that we don't even notice it happening.

But one day, we look back at an old photo and our breath gets caught in our throat.

Somehow, that little baby turned into a toddler, and is now a kid.

It all happens so fast.

For today, pause and pay attention.

Really look at them.

Commit what you see and hear to your memory.

You'll want to remember every little detail one day.

LETTER #100

FOR YOU, WHEN YOU REALIZE EVEN THOUGH YOU ARE TIRED AND WEARY, YOU WOULDN'T TRADE IT FOR THE WORLD

Dear Mama,

Raising a child is the most demanding, exhausting, fascinating, and thrilling job on the planet.

At least, it is to those of us who decided to become parents.

We are raising up the next generation of humans who will occupy planet Earth.

We are raising up the next generation who will one day lead our government, military, and society.

We are raising up the future of the human race.

What is more important or powerful than that?

Being a mother is hard.

Being a mother is exhausting.

Being a mother can drain your energy, and zap your patience in a way nothing else can.

It's often thankless, isolating, frustrating, and sometimes just plain gross.

But, being a mother is also the most magical gift.

Being a mother is fulfilling, rewarding, and remarkable.

It stretches you in ways you never imagined - literally and figuratively.

It brings new life where there previously was none, and allows you to witness the growth of a human right before your very eyes.

It gives you a blessedly precious chance to see life through the eyes of a child again.

It fills you with more love than you ever believed possible.

No matter how frustrated, irritated, isolated, or angry parenting makes you...

No matter how anxious, worried, emotional, or just plain exhausted you are...

Being your child's mother is worth all of it.

Every sleepless night, every diaper blowout.

Every vegetable refused, every toy bin dumped.

Every tear, every outburst, every consequence.

Every single frustration and hard part is worth it because you also get to experience the love.

The hugs, the kisses, the snuggles, the laughs.

The new experiences, the magical wonder, the childlike innocence.

The core memories, the newfound hobbies, the major milestones.

You get to experience, nurture, and witness your child's life, as they are born and grow.

What a magical miraculous privilege it is.

It is worth every single hard thing to get to be their mother.

Their safe place.

Their home.

Their mama.

Afterword

I wrote this book for you, and I also wrote it for me.

I wrote it for the pre-baby version of me who was unsure, scared, and cautiously excited to become a mother.

I wrote it for the postpartum version of me who was healing from an unexpected c-section while learning to care for a newborn.

I wrote it for the sleep deprived, hormonal version of me that felt off balance and disoriented in the early months of motherhood.

I wrote it for the version of myself that felt completely alone as I rocked my new son to sleep in the middle of the night.

These letters are the words I wish could have read when I was a new mother.

They are the encouragement, camaraderie, and perspective that I so desperately wanted and needed in those early days of motherhood.

It is my sincere hope that you are comforted, encouraged, and lifted up by the letters in this book.

I'm cheering you on and rooting for you.

xo, Laura Radniecki

P.S. If the words in this book spoke to your heart, I would love to hear about it. I humbly ask you to consider leaving a review so I can read about the ways this book encouraged and inspired you.

As we all know, reviews are what people use to decide to buy anything, so your kind words will help get this book in front of new mamas who desperately need the support and love found in these pages.

Thank you, and I'm truly grateful for you.

Get FREE
Phone Wallpapers

Download beautiful phone wallpapers FREE, so you can carry the encouragement of **Dear Mama** with you, wherever you go!

Scan the icon below with your phone's camera to sign up and get your free backgrounds.

http://bit.ly/3kvwzJF